Ripley's OCEANS®

Believe It or Not!

RIPLEY
PUBLISHING

a Jim Pattison Company

TWISTS

Written by Camilla de la Bedoyere
Consultant Barbara Taylor

RIPLEY PUBLISHING

Publisher Anne Marshall

Editorial Director Rebecca Miles
Project Editor Lisa Regan
Editorial Assistant Charlotte Howell
Picture Researchers James Proud, Charlotte Howell
Proofreader Judy Barratt
Indexer Hilary Bird

Art Director Sam South
Senior Designer Michelle Cannatella
Design Rocket Design (East Anglia) Ltd
Reprographics Juice Creative Ltd

www.ripleybooks.com

For information regarding permission, write to VP Intellectual Property, Ripley Entertainment Inc., Suite 188, 7576 Kingspointe Parkway, Orlando, Florida 32819
email: publishing@ripleys.com

Library of Congress Cataloging-in-Publication Data is available.

Manufactured in China
in May/2011 by Leo Paper
2nd printing

PUBLISHER'S NOTE
While every effort has been made to verify the accuracy of the entries in this book, the Publishers cannot be held responsible for any errors contained in the work. They would be glad to receive any information from readers.

WARNING
Some of the stunts and activities in this book are undertaken by experts and should not be attempted by anyone without adequate training and supervision.

CONTENTS

TWISTS

MAKING A SPLASH

Have you ever gazed out at the ocean and wondered what lies beneath? Well, wonder no more. Take an ocean trip without getting your hair wet, and dip a toe into the great sea of knowledge!

Two-thirds of our planet is water, and the five great oceans are full of more creatures than any other place on Earth. From the sunny shallows to the dark and dingy depths, this book will bring you face to face with marine mammals, deep sea divers, and lots and lots of fish. Come on… dive in!

WHAT'S INSIDE YOUR BOOK?

ALL CHANGE

This octopus is called the "day octopus" because it hunts in the day. As such it needs to be a camouflage expert, so it can hunt successfully, and not be hunted. It is usually brown but can change color as it swims from sand and rocks to coral. One marine biologist reported seeing an individual day octopus changing color and patterns 1,000 times in seven hours.

It is one of the largest octopus species, with tentacles 30 inches long.

Learn fab facts to go with the cool pictures.

The day octopus is sometimes called the big blue octopus.

Some colors allow "false eye" spots to be seen in its pattern, near its tentacles.

TWISTS

BLUE WHALE
The world's largest ever creature, a blue whale eats about 4 tons of krill (a tiny shrimplike sea creature) every day.
Size: 80–100 feet

THRESHER SHARK
A thresher shark can leap right out of the water. Its tail is often half the length of its body.
Size: 10–16½ feet

SEA LION
A California sea lion dives for up to five minutes, but can hunt non-stop for up to 30 hours.
Size: 5½–7¼ feet

Big Word Alert! Don't be put off by the big words—they're all explained here.

Ripley explains...

Ripley explains some of the science and know-how from oceanic experts.

GOOD REEF

COOL CORALS

Coral reefs lie in the shimmering blue waters of coastal areas. They make up just one percent of all ocean habitats, but these natural places are home to [...] percent of all marine animals and plants.

You may think of a coral reef as a rocky place underwater, but it is much more than that. Inside each reef there are [...]illions of mini-builders called polyps. [The]se soft-bodied animals build rocky cups [arou]nd their soft bodies. Over thousands [of y]ears, the cups create an enormous, [...] structure—the reef itself—and this [becom]es a giant ecosystem where a huge [vari]ety of living things exist together.

[The]re are many [dif]ferent types of [co]ral, and some of [th]em have names [th]at describe their [a]ppearance perfectly!

ECOSYSTEM
This is a place, such as a rainforest or coral reef, and includes all the animals and plants that live in it and interact with each other.

BIG WORD ALERT

STAGHORN CORAL

STAR CORAL

FAN CORAL

[...] CORAL

BRAIN CORAL

MUSHROOM CORAL

twist it!

Some types of coral can survive in deep, dark, and cold water. There may be more coldwater coral reefs than warm ones.

The most famous reef is the Great Barrier Reef in Australia's waters. It isn't actually just one reef, but a group of around 3,000 reefs and 1,000 small islands that spread nearly 1,250 miles.

Most coral polyps are colonial animals, which means they live together in big groups. They don't always get on, and if there is not much space one polyp might lean over and kill its next-door neighbor!

REEF RICHES
The Coral Triangle is a huge area of sea around Indonesia and Malaysia with many types of fish live there. More than 3,000 coral islands and reefs.

Ripley's Believe It or Not!

Coral kids

These figures are part of an underwater sculpture museum created by a London artist named Jason de Caires Taylor. Jason's artwork is designed to encourage the growth of new corals.

15

Look for the Ripley "R" to find out even more than you knew before!

These books are all about "Believe It or Not!"— amazing facts, feats, and things that will make you go "Wow!"

PELICAN
Pelicans can eat 2 pounds of fish each day and can swallow a fish that is 1½ feet long.
Size: 3⅓–6 feet

LOBSTER
The biggest lobster ever caught was nearly 4 feet long. It was caught in Nova Scotia, Canada, and was probably over 100 years old.
Size: up to 3¼ feet

SEAHORSE
Seahorses need to eat nearly all the time to stay alive. They have no teeth and no stomach.
Size: 0.6–14 inches

WILD WIND AND WAVES

WORLD WEATHER

<< Turn the tide >>

Ever wondered where weather comes from, and if the weather, wind, waves, and warm air are all connected? The answer is yes! The world's weather is all down to the ways that the Sun, the Earth, its oceans, and the atmosphere work together.

The way that ocean water can move closer to, or further away from a coastline is called a tide. Tides happen twice a day in most places and are caused by the way the Moon's gravity pulls on the Earth. In Nova Scotia, Canada, the difference between the ocean's depth at low tides and high tides can reach nearly 50 feet: that is the height of eight men standing on top of one another!

Oceans are giant weather-makers and climate-shakers. They control the planet's atmosphere and temperature, and our seasons, winds, and rains. Ocean water collects heat around the Equator, and moves it as far as the Poles—keeping most of the world warm enough for living things to exist. Warm wet air collects over the oceans as clouds and travels to land, where it falls as rain.

BIG WORD ALERT

ATMOSPHERE
The thick layer of gases, including the oxygen we breathe, that surrounds the Earth. The atmosphere plays a big part in the world's weather.

ALL AT SEA

- Waves are caused by wind moving the surface of the ocean. As they approach land, where the water gets shallow, waves move more slowly, but they can become taller.

- A wave at sea is called a swell and the largest ones ever measured reached over 100 feet from their troughs (bottoms) to their crests (tops).

- Broken wave patterns might mean deadly rip currents. These currents can pull even the strongest swimmers out to sea, so never swim without an adult's supervision.

Icebergs are giant blocks of floating ice that form in the cold polar regions. Oil companies use boats and ropes to move them when they want to explore the seafloor below!

<< Spiral storm >>

Warm ocean water creates hurricanes by heating air. The warm air starts to swirl, creating winds that become giant storms. When they move onto land, hurricane winds, heavy rain, and a rapid rise in sea level (a storm surge) cause devastation in coastal areas. Hurricanes are also called tropical cyclones or typhoons in the western Pacific Ocean.

The middle of a hurricane is fairly calm and is called "the eye."

Ripley explains...

Cloud formation

Rain

Water vapor

Water runs back to the ocean

Ocean

THE WATER CYCLE

Oceans are a major part of the whole world's water system, which is called the global water cycle. Rainwater flows from land to the oceans, and when ocean water is heated it evaporates to form clouds.

OCEAN MOTION

OUT OF SIGHT

Beneath the gently slurping, swelling surface of the oceans, there is a whole other world waiting to be explored. Imagine you are about to dive all the way to the bottom of the sea... you're embarking on a perilous journey.

You travel through the light zones, where sunlight still reaches, and shoals of fish swim past. As you dive deeper, you notice the darkness, and the deathly cold and quiet around you. There are few signs of life. On the ocean floor, your feet sink into deep squashy mud and sludge.

BIG WORD ALERT

MARINE
This word is used to describe anything to do with seas and oceans.

Deep diver

William Trubridge is a top free-diver. In this extreme sport, people descend as far as they can below the surface of the sea on a single breath of air. In 2009, William reached a lung-crunching depth of 288 feet 8 inches.

Tsunami power

These images show the movement of water during the 2004 Indian Ocean tsunami, at Kalutara in Sri Lanka. The top picture shows the normal level of the ocean. Then, just before the tsunami hit, the water pulled back from the shoreline, and then swirled across roads and houses. This tsunami killed over 200,000 people in 14 countries.

Normal level

Water recedes

Tsunami hits

Upward wave

Crust

FAULT LINE

Mantle

The Earth's surface is broken into tectonic plates, which move all the time. When they move suddenly they can cause an earthquake, which pushes a surge of water (a tsunami) onto land. Tsunamis can wipe out entire towns and villages.

Where plates move against one another, mountains and volcanoes can form. The peak of Mauna Kea in Hawaii is the top of an underwater mountain, which is higher than Everest.

WATER WORLD

Rivers of water, called currents, flow within oceans. The global conveyor is an enormous system of currents that travels around all the oceans. It takes seawater to move around the Earth.

Ocean water contains "marine snow," which is made of clumps of bits of dead animals, plants, and poo. Living things feed on marine snow, which floats down to the seabed at a rate of 656 feet a day.

The strongest current in the world is in the Southern Ocean, between South America and Antarctica. Water flows here at an incredible rate of over 4½ million cubic feet per second.

Twist it!

Seawater is packed with minerals, including salts. Salt makes seawater very dense (see page 17). Just one bathtub of seawater contains about 6¼ pounds of salt!

Small amounts of gold and copper are also found in the oceans.

Ocean water contains gases, such as oxygen and carbon dioxide, that have dissolved into it. Marine animals and plants need these gases to survive.

A helping flipper

Sea lions are so smart that the US Navy has recruited them to help guard deep-diving bots. These mine-hunting mammals can learn how underwater equipment works and attach cables to them, so they can be pulled to the surface.

GROW ZONE

As oceans are the world's biggest habitat it's no wonder they teem with life. There are more living things in ocean waters than anywhere else, and the biggest variety live near the surface.

The reasons for this are simple: in the top 650 feet of water (known as the Sunlight Zone) there is light, warmth, and plenty of food—what more could anyone ask for? This region is like the farms or rainforests of the oceans, where food for ocean animals grows. Shallow areas around land are called coasts and they are particularly busy places.

BIG WORD ALERT

HABITAT
The place where a plant or animal naturally lives and grows.

Marvelous mussels!

Rivers flow into the coastal areas, bringing lots of fresh water and food, making these places especially good habitats. Some coastal plants and animals, such as these mussels, have to be able to survive underwater, when the tide is in, and in air when the tide goes out.

First swim of the day, lovely!

Played hide and seek in the water

Met up with the gang. More swimming...

A DAY IN THE LIFE...

Sea otters like to snooze in coastal kelp forests because the seaweed stops them from floating away in their sleep. These marine animals are smart—they lie on their backs and use stones to smash open crabs and shells they have balanced on their bellies!

A shellfish snack while swimming.

Coast

Ocean

Continental shelf

Continental slope

TAKING A DIP

The continental shelf is where land slopes gently into the sea. Light can pass through the water here, right down to the seabed. That's why shallow areas in the sea are called the Sunlight Zone.

Ripley's Believe It or Not!®

Little archer fish catch flying insects by spitting at them! When a stunned insect falls into the water, the smart fish gobbles it up.

GOTCHA!

Sea trees

In some warm places, mangrove trees grow along coasts to create mangrove swamps. Strangely, these trees don't mind salty seawater and they make unique habitats. More than half the world's mangrove swamps have been destroyed in recent times, to make room for fish and shrimp farms.

FEELING WEEDY

Seaweeds are not like other plants—they're slimy! The slime stops other animals from settling on them, and keeps them from drying out at low tide.

Tiny animals and plants, called plankton, drift along in the ocean's Sunlight Zone. They are the food of many other animals. A large whale can eat more than 5,000 pounds of plankton in a day.

We use seaweed as food and to make medicines, cosmetics (make-up), paint, glue, and paper.

Brown seaweeds are called kelp and they used to be burned to make soap. Kelp can grow as enormous underwater forests and some types can grow 1–2 feet a day.

twist it!

COASTAL CROCS

Gharials are slender-jawed relatives of crocodiles. They live in coastal waters around India, but they will probably be extinct in the wild soon. There are only about 200 left.

ANIMALS IN ARMOR

SAFETY SUITS

If you've got a soft, spongy body, what's the best way to protect yourself from predators? Many small marine animals have got the perfect answer—they wear armor. This armor is like a super-strong skin and it's packed with tough minerals that make it hard. A crustacean's armor is called a carapace, but mollusks grow shells.

Sea urchins and starfish hide their armor under a thin layer of colorful skin. They have skeletons made up of interlocking plates of calcium— the strong mineral that's in our bones and teeth. The animals in this group have their mouths on their bottoms and tiny suckers called feet!

Ripley explains...

Lobsters, crabs, prawns, shrimp, and krill are all **crustaceans**.

Clams, oysters, mussels, dog whelks, and cowries are all **mollusks**.

COCONUT SHY

This veined octopus doesn't grow tough armor, so he made his own out of a coconut shell. He can close the shell when he wants to hide, but when it's time to make a quick getaway he grabs it with his eight tentacles, and runs for it!

Japanese giant

This colossal crustacean's Japanese name means "tall-leg." No prizes for guessing why! The largest Japanese spider crab ever recorded measured an enormous 145 1/4 inches from the tip of one leg to another. And some fishermen swear they've seen crabs that are nearly double that size!

twist it!

When Paul Westlake lost his wallet in the ocean, he thought he'd seen the last of it. A few days later, however, a deep-sea diver found the missing wallet in the clutches of a large lobster!

Razor clams can dig themselves into the seabed at a super-speedy rate of 1 inch every second. Scientists have copied their technique, and built a digging robot called RoboClam.

SO SHELLFISH

Scaly-foot snails have ultra-tough armor. Their shells are so strong that scientists are studying them to find out how to make better armor for soldiers and vehicles. The secret lies in the snails' three-layer shells, which are strengthened with iron.

ARMY OF ARMS

Three five-armed starfish devour a dead fish. Like heavily armored tanks, the animals can munch away, protected from predators by their tough outer skins.

CRAB RACING

Meet the elite sports stars of the crab world. These hermit crabs have undergone thorough fitness training to reach their peak, and are primed and ready to race. These little athletes compete for the National Crab Racing Association, based in Florida, and after six months they retire in style, to spend their remaining days in the lap of luxury as pampered pets.

Watch out!

Sea urchins don't have eyes, which might be why this little guy didn't spot the giant sea snail approaching! Sea urchins have spiky spines, but they are still no match for this mighty mollusk.

GOOD REEF
COOL CORALS

Coral reefs lie in the shimmering blue waters of coastal areas. They make up just one percent of all ocean habitats, but these natural places are home to 25 percent of all marine animals and plants.

You may think of a coral reef as a rocky place underwater, but it is much more than that. Inside each reef there are millions of mini-builders called polyps. These soft-bodied animals build rocky cups around their soft bodies. Over thousands of years, the cups create an enormous, solid structure—the reef itself—and this becomes a giant ecosystem where a huge variety of living things exist together.

BIG WORD ALERT

ECOSYSTEM
This is a place, such as a rainforest or coral reef, and includes all the animals and plants that live in it and interact with each other.

STAR CORAL

FINGER CORAL

BRAIN CORAL

There are many different types of coral, and some of them have names that describe their appearance perfectly!

STAGHORN CORAL

Some types of coral can survive in deep, dark, and cold water. There may be more coldwater coral reefs than warm ones.

The most famous reef is the Great Barrier Reef in Australia's waters. It isn't actually just one reef, but a group of around 3,000 reefs and 1,000 small islands that spread nearly 1,250 miles.

Most coral polyps are colonial animals, which means they live together in big groups. They don't always get on, and if there is not much space one polyp might lean over and kill its next-door neighbor!

The Coral Triangle is a huge area of sea around Indonesia and Malaysia with many coral islands and reefs. More than 3,000 types of fish live there.

REEF RICHES

FAN CORAL

Ripley's
Believe It or Not!®

Coral kids

These figures are part of an underwater sculpture museum created by a London artist named Jason de Caires Taylor. Jason's artwork is designed to encourage the growth of new corals.

MUSHROOM CORAL

SUPERSIZE SEA

Enormous eye

The colossal squid of the Southern Ocean has the biggest eyes of any living animal. Each eyeball can measure nearly 10 inches across and—no surprises here—it has fantastic eyesight, even though it can't see anything in color.

In 2007, fishermen in the Antarctic seas caught a colossal squid that was 33 feet long and weighed nearly 1,000 pounds. That's more than twice the weight of a large male gorilla.

ACTUAL SIZE!

almost 10 inches wide!

When it comes to surviving undersea, size really matters. Being big has one major advantage—it's much harder for other things to catch and eat you!

Seawater is denser than freshwater, or air. That means the particles, or molecules, inside it are packed tightly together, and can hold up objects in it. That's why we can float quite easily in seawater. Things feel lighter in seawater than they do in air, because the water pushes up underneath them and supports their weight. That means ocean animals can grow much bigger than those on land. Floating in seawater may be easy, but moving through it takes lots of energy. So, marine monsters often travel with ocean currents.

Ripley's Believe It or Not!®

The oceans are full of worms that burrow into the seafloor, or live inside another animal. The longest in the world are boot-lace worms, which live in the North Sea. They can grow to 100 feet long!

Mega yuck!

Giant clam

Giant clams can measure more than 3 feet across. They live around coral reefs and get food from the water, or from tiny algae that live on the edges of their shells. It is thought they can live to 100 years of age, or even longer.

BIG BLUE BABY

A blue whale calf is one-and-a-half times the length of an average-sized car when it is born. Blue whales are the world's largest animals, so it's no wonder they have big bouncing babies! They weigh up to 3 tons at birth—that's the same as 882 human newborns. Once born, the baby (which is known as a calf) drinks over 400 pints of its mother's milk every day.

Blue whales produce monster-sized pink poo! Each poo is nearly 10 inches wide and many feet long! The strange color comes from krill, the little shrimp-like animals the whales eat.

What's in a name?

Some fish get their names from the way they look. Would you kiss one of these—even if it was called "sweetlips"?

ANGEL FISH

HARLEQUIN SWEETLIPS

MASKED BUTTERFLY FISH

SOMETHING FISHY

MASTERS **OF THE SEA**

Fish have been around for a very long time: more than 500 million years! The oceans and seas are now home to zillions of them, and there are more and there are more fish in the world than any other type of vertebrate.

Fish are the masters of the sea, but what's the secret to their success? Being able to breathe underwater has got to be one big advantage! A backbone helps, too—it gives an animal something to build its muscles and organs around, and connects the brain to all the other body bits. Fish were the first creatures on Earth to develop a backbone, and it was so successful that all of us other vertebrates then copied this brilliant design.

BIG WORD ALERT

VERTEBRATE
An animal with a backbone. Fish, birds, reptiles, amphibians, and mammals are vertebrates.

School meals

The super-talented sailfish has an amazing way of dining out. Several of smaller fish, like sardines or sailfish shepherd together schools anchovies, into a "baitball," and then use their high fins to create a wall to stop their prey from escaping.

PARROT FISH

PINEAPPLE FISH

TRUMPETFISH

Ripley's Believe It or Not!®

FAT FISH

The small fish at the top is an aptly named "great swallower" fish. It was found in the Cayman Islands having somehow eaten a snake mackerel five times bigger!

A fish's body is built for life underwater. That usually means a body shape that is streamlined (the best shape for swimming, with fins and tails.)

Clowning around

All fish, including these clownfish, can breathe because they have special organs called gills, which take dissolved oxygen out of the water.

TOO COOL FOR SCHOOL

A group of fish is called a school or shoal. Millions of herrings get together to make giant, swarming shoals when it is time to spawn (lay their eggs). It's often safer to travel in a group!

Orange roughies don't look remarkable, but these deep-sea swimmers have been known to live to well over 100 years old—making them one of the longest-lived of all fish.

A group of eels is called a seething, a group of herrings is called an army, and a group of sharks is called a shiver.

Many fish have swim bladders that stop them from sinking. When gas goes into a swim bladder, the fish can move up in the water; when gas passes out of it, the fish can sink deeper.

twist it!

FAST, FURIOUS, FREAKY

BIODIVERSITY RULES OK

From flesh-sucking lampreys to four-eyed ghostly spookfish, there is an enormous range of fish in our oceans.

There are fish to suit almost every habitat, from rock pools at the seaside to the dark depths, and every way of life. There are hiders and fighters, swimmers and flyers, flat fish and fat fish, angry fish and clown fish—there are even fish with giant fangs, enormous mouths, or poisonous spines. There are also some frankly weird fish out there, too.

Fast!

What a sucker!

This lovely lamprey is like a long, bendy hosepipe, with a scrubbing brush at the end. It attaches itself to its prey with a sucker-mouth while rows of tiny rasping teeth scrape away at the flesh. This hungry fella then sucks it up, with a side order of oozing blood. Yum!

Hey, suckers!

WATCH OUT!

- Barracudas are big (up to 6 feet in length) and they are smart. They chase their prey into shallow water and start to feed. Once they are full, the barracudas save the rest for later. They work together to guard their prey and stop them escaping!

- Eating barracudas is a risky business, because they eat fish that feed on poisonous algae. If you feast on an affected fish you could suffer deadly food poisoning.

WHO YOU LOOKING AT?

Male garibaldis are furious little fish, with bad tempers. They grind their teeth and have been known to attack divers! If there are too many males in a group, some of them change into females.

Furious!

WEIRD AND WONDERFUL

Titan triggerfish don't like people one bit. These large fish attack divers and have a poisonous bite. They've even walloped divers so hard they've passed out!

Tuna fish never stop swimming. They keep moving at a rate of around 4 miles an hour for their entire lives. A 15-year-old tuna has probably swum about half a million miles!

When a female jawfish has laid her eggs, she scoots off and leaves the dad to take over. He keeps them in his mouth until they are ready to hatch.

Baby halibut look perfectly normal, but they morph into freaky flatfish as they grow. One eye moves across its head and joins the other one on the right-hand side, which becomes the top. The mouth twists round to the fish's left side, which turns into its underbelly.

Twist it!

MR BLOBBY

Meet the blobfish: blob by name and slob by nature! These soft and squidgy creatures live in the deep waters around Australia, and they like a lazy life. Females sit on the ocean floor when protecting their eggs, but the rest of the time blobfish hover just above the seabed, mooching around and waiting for lunch to pass by.

Freaky!

Up, up, and away!

Flying fish escape predators by leaping out of the water and gliding just above the waves. They can travel through the air for up to 40 seconds and cover around 150 feet.

MEGAMOUTHS

SHARK ATTACK!

Of all the world's creatures, sharks are among the most feared. Their incredible speed, cold black eyes, and rows of killer teeth set in enormous jaws have these sleek swimmers marked out as terrifying predators.

SOME-FIN SPECIAL

The megamouth is really a type of shark. It has a huge mouth, but eats tiny creatures such as plankton and jellyfish.

The smallest sharks are dwarf lantern sharks, which are usually 6–7 inches long.

A shark's body is covered in teeth rather than scales! Denticles are growths from the skin that are made of enamel (the same hard substance that's in teeth).

Tiger sharks eat almost anything: fish, squid, sea snakes, seals, birds, and stingrays... they have also been found with old tires, trash, and car license plates in their stomachs!

twist it!

Ripley explains...

Sharks usually have dark backs. This camouflages them against the dark water when seen from above. They are pale underneath, which helps them to remain invisible when viewed from below, against a pale sky. The same type of coloring is used in fighter planes.

Whale shark

Whale sharks are the largest fish in the world and can grow to over 40 feet long. They feed on tiny animals by opening their enormous mouths and sucking in water and food. This means that, if one swims near you, it's safe to stop and enjoy the view! In fact, as far as most sharks are concerned, you wouldn't make good grub. Nearly all sharks have no interest in attacking and eating humans.

We may fear sharks, but the truth is we know very little about them. There could be more than 500 different types of shark, with many of those still waiting to be discovered in the depths of the ocean. Lots of sharks are hunters, but the largest ones actually feed on shoals of tiny krill and other small animals. While some lay eggs, a [...] sharks are [...] to give birth to live young.

TOP 5 KILLER SHARKS

1. Great white
2. Tiger
3. Bull
4. Requiem
5. Sandtiger

TOP 3 SURVIVAL TIPS

Fight back: punch the shark on the snout—hard!

Stick your fingers in its eyes and gills.

Get out of the water!

Sharks, skates, and rays don't have bones—their skeletons are made of cartilage instead. Cartilage is more flexible than bone, and it's the same stuff that makes your nose and ears stiff.

Ripley's Believe It or Not!®

Life saver

Free diver Craig Clasen had to wrestle with a 12-foot tiger shark to save the life of his friend Ryan. An experienced diver, he recognized that the shark was hungry and highly dangerous. It took him two hours to fight off the shark, and he even tried to drown it.

Great white shark

- Baby great white sharks measure about 5 feet when they're born.
- A baby must leave its mother straightaway or it might get eaten!
- An adult can swim up to 25 mph.
- Great white sharks can vomit up their entire stomachs. It's a good way to clear out rubbish and bones and avoid an upset tummy!

WATER WINGS

Some birds swoop and soar over the oceans for months at a time. Others prefer to paddle at the seaside, pecking at tasty worms and shellfish. Penguins, however, are supreme marine birds—they are so well suited to ocean life that they have even lost the power of flight, and use their wings like flippers instead.

BLUE SHOES

This little fella is a little blue penguin called Elvis—and he's got blue shoes! He lives at the International Antarctic Centre in Christchurch, New Zealand, with several of his friends, who all wear shoes to protect their feet. They have developed sore feet after standing around much more than they would do in the wild, where they swim almost constantly.

SUN SUIT

Pierre the African penguin has his own wet suit! His friends at the California Academy of Sciences in San Francisco gradually lose their feathers to grow shiny new ones, but Pierre loses so many that he needs his suit to keep him warm, and to stop him from getting sunburn.

Watch the birdie

Marine birds have bodies suited for swimming and diving. Many have webbed feet, waterproof feathers, and special glands that help them deal with salt. Some birds fly over water, diving into the oceans to grab food. Others live on the coasts and feed on animals living in muddy seashores.

Male blue-footed boobies strut around in front of females, showing off their lovely webbed toes. The brighter the blue, the more the females are impressed!

Common guillemots lay eggs with very pointed ends. This shape stops the eggs from rolling off the cliff edges where the birds nest.

Herring gulls can be aggressive, and have been known to attack people and dogs.

BLUE-FOOTED BOOBIE

COMMON GUILLEMOT

HERRING GULL

The oceans contain fish, so it's no wonder that birds have adapted to be able to pluck these protein-packed snacks out of the salty water. No birds, however, have been able to become totally marine animals, because they all have to return to land to lay their eggs.

MASSIVE WINGSPAN — AS LONG AS A SMALL CAR...

....WOW!

Wandering albatrosses have the biggest wingspan of any bird: 11½ feet—that's longer than two adult bikes! They live at sea, snatching squid from the water, and can fly for several weeks at a time without ever landing.

CATCH A WAVE

Surfing is a real action sport, and it's even better when you don't need a board! Gentoo penguins in the Falkland Islands know just where to go to get the best waves, and surf barefoot into shore. They even swim back out again to have another turn!

Ripley's— Believe It or Not!

Pelicans have enormous throat pouches, which they use to scoop up water: as much as 3 gallons at a time. They tip their heads back to drain out the water, and gobble up any fish.

Puffins are sometimes called sea parrots, because of their startling appearance. They spend most of their time at sea, occasionally diving to grab small fish.

Skuas have gross eating habits. They chase other sea birds and scare them into vomiting up their food—which the skuas then gobble up!

PUFFIN

PELICAN

SKUA

MARINE MAMMALS

ALL AT SEA

When life on land got too tough, some mammals headed back to the water. Whales, dolphins, seals, walruses, and dugongs are all descended from land-living beasts that decided, millions of years ago, that swimming is more fun than walking!

This devotion to the ocean was handy, because it meant marine mammals were able to escape from their predators, and find new sources of food: fish, krill, or seagrass. There were some major downsides though—they still had to breathe air, and life in water required new body shapes, less fur, and better ways to keep warm in the icy depths.

Polar bears

Polar bears have super-sensitive hearing and can detect seals swimming below ice that is 3-feet thick! Their sense of smell is impressive too—these giant bears can sniff the whiff of rotting meat 3 miles away. They dive into the water and bear-paddle their way to find lunch. They can swim for 60 miles without stopping!

KEY FACTS

- All marine mammals breathe air, but they have evolved (changed over time) to spend a long time underwater before needing to breathe again.

- Whales, dolphins, and porpoises belong to a group of mammals called cetaceans (say: set-aysh-uns). They give birth underwater and usually have just one baby at a time.

- The skeletons of marine mammals show they are descended from land-living animals that had four limbs.

Walrus

Male walruses can grow enormous teeth (called tusks) of 20 inches or more. They use the tusks to pull themselves onto slabs of ice and as lethal weapons when they fight one another.

Marine mammals may not be covered in fur, but they do have some sprouts of hair, such as whiskers. Young marine mammals usually have more hair than adults.

DOLPHINS

Dolphins play bubble hoopla! These clever creatures can create bubbles with air from their blowholes and swim through them. They like to make different shapes and sizes—just for fun!

Swimmers are sometimes surprised to find themselves surrounded by dolphins slapping their tails and circling. The dolphins aren't just being friendly—they are keeping prowling sharks away. No one knows why dolphins protect humans in this way.

twist it!

A blue whale's tongue weighs as much as a whole elephant!

Beluga whales are called sea canaries because they sing so sweetly.

Cetaceans are smart and can talk to each other. Humpback whales make the longest, most complicated sounds of any animal. They sing by forcing air through their nose.

Cetaceans and seals swim with their muscular tails, while sea lions use their front flippers.

IN THE SWIM

Elephant seals

Elephant seals can dive to depths of more than 3,000 feet and can wait for two hours between breaths. Their hearts beat very slowly when they dive, to save energy.

BIG WORD ALERT

MAMMAL
These animals have hair or fur and give birth to live young, which they feed with their own milk.

LOOK AT ME

There's an underwater beauty parade of animals that like to razzle, dazzle, dance, and display. Animals living in the Sunlight Zone (see page 10) get the full benefit of being in the spotlight, so they are more likely to show off with extraordinary colors and patterns than those who live in deeper, darker water. Light rays dance off their shimmering scales, patterned skins, and colored shells— what a sight!

Attention-seekers use their good looks to impress mates, or to warn predators to stay away. The shy and retiring types prefer to dress down and use colors and patterns to hide in dappled, shallow waters.

Harlequin shrimp

Some shrimps can change color to blend in with their surroundings, but harlequin shrimps are already perfect. Their brightly colored patches may not look like an ideal type of camouflage, but when they are hidden in the shadows, the patterns help disguise the shrimp's outline. The harlequin shrimps then emerge to attack starfish, which they catch and eat alive, arm by arm.

Mandarin fish are among the most beautiful of all reef fish, but their glorious neon colors are not there to impress. They warn potential predators of a foul-tasting slime that covers the fish's body.

MANDARIN FISH

Seafood salad

What would you call a crab that looks like a strawberry? A strawberry crab, of course! This tasty-looking fella has only been recently discovered, off the coast of Taiwan. Scientists are trying to find out why a crab would want to look like a strawberry. If they can find others that look like grapes, bananas, and oranges they plan to make a delicious crab fruit salad!

Ripley's Believe It or Not!®

28

CANDY FLATWORM

Some sea creatures like bold and brash looks, while others prefer the delicate and dainty approach. Candy flatworms hide their gentle beauty under rocks, until it's time to brave the waters and seek food. They glide smoothly along the seabed, or swim just above it.

Isn't this jellyfish gorgeous, with its lovely floaty body, pretty color, and little spots? At night these mauve stingers become even more attractive, because their bodies pulse with light as they are carried along by the currents. They may be good-looking, but these are jellyfish you wouldn't want to bump into—they are covered in stinging cells!

Color is created by pigments, which are in the outer layer of the animal's body. This outer layer may be skin, scales, or tough shells. Some deep-sea marine animals have colorful bacteria on their skin, or bacteria that produce light, for an extra-special spectacle.

I can't believe you're wearing the same as me tonight!

Dragon moray eels may have splendid colors, stripes, and spots, but they like to keep their beauty well hidden. They lurk in the shadows, and come out only at night.

BIG WORD ALERT

CAMOUFLAGE
The way an animal uses color and patterns to hide.

INTO THE ABYSS

DEEP** AND **DARK*

This habitat is so hostile that humans can only travel here in submersibles. So far, just two brave explorers have ever reached the deep ocean floor 6¾ miles down—that's fewer than have been to the Moon and back! This underwater world is not empty of life, though. Weird and wonderful creatures have made a home in the depths. Many of them feed on marine snow (see page 9) and the remains of dead animals that have sunk to the seabed.

If you could swim to the deepest parts of the ocean, you would be squashed to death in an instant by the huge weight of water above and around you. Sunlight can't reach the deep, and an eerie gloom takes over in the inky darkness.

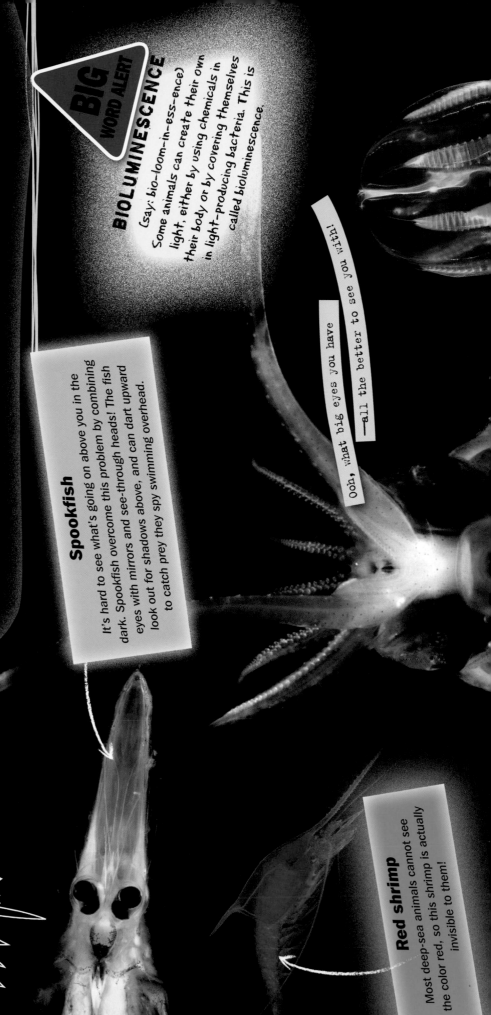

BIG WORD ALERT

BIOLUMINESCENCE

(say: bio-loom-in-ess-ence) Some animals can create their own light, either by using chemicals in their body or by covering themselves in light-producing bacteria. This is called bioluminescence.

Spookfish

It's hard to see what's going on above you in the dark. Spookfish overcome this problem by combining see-through heads! The fish eyes with mirrors and see-through eyes with mirrors above, and can dart upward look out for shadows above, and can dart upward to catch prey they spy swimming overhead.

Ooh, what big eyes you have —all the better to see you with!

Red shrimp

Most deep-sea animals cannot see the color red, so this shrimp is actually invisible to them!

SINK TO THE BOTTOM

Colossal squid are so big their eyes are as large as dinner plates (see page 16). Big eyes are handy in the Twilight Zone, where a little light still reaches.

Ugly hagfish are covered in slime that sometimes gets up their nose and makes them sneeze! To stop this happening, they tie a knot in their own body and force the body downward, squeezing the slime away!

Hot water gushes out of the ocean floor in some places, and living things thrive in the warmth. These hydrothermal vents are home to giant tube worms nearly 8 feet long.

Sperm whales have ribs that fold and collapse when they dive. Their lungs scrunch up, too. They can store oxygen in their muscles for more than 30 minutes and can swim to depths of nearly 5,000 feet.

twist it!

Comb jelly

Comb jellies are covered in rows of tiny hairs called cilia. When their cilia move, they shimmer with bright colors. They trap their prey with sticky slime on their tentacles.

Cockatoo squid

The curious-looking cockatoo squid swims with its tentacles delicately arranged above its head—it's a good look!

A bit of wind helps a cockatoo squid to float up and down. They use this gas-filled organ to move and swim!

Anglerfish

An anglerfish hides its dark body in lights in front of its head. The lure deep, but suspends a tantalizing attracting prey toward the angler's gaping jaws.

HUNT HIDE OR

FEEDING ****TIME****

Food is energy—energy to grow, move, mate, and have young, and to eat even more food! Marine animals, just like those on land, have to spend lots of their time finding food. They also have to try their best not to become someone else's meal!

Animals that hunt others are called predators. They mostly need strength, speed, and great senses to find food. The lunch-bunch that get eaten are called prey, and their job is to hide, fight back, or fool predators into thinking they are something else completely. These crafty creatures have got some clever strategies up their sleeves!

Power puff

When a porcupine fish is scared, it hides in caves. If there's nowhere to hide, it fills its body up with water and swells to the size of a prickly football.

HIDE

Wolf fish

This ferocious-looking fish is called a wolf fish, because of its dog-like teeth. It lurks in dark corners and emerges only when it is hungry. Wolf fish like to exercise their jaws on crunchy shellfish, crabs, and sea urchins. Every year they grow new teeth to replace the ones destroyed by all that munching.

HUNT

Leaf me alone

Leafy seadragons are masters of disguise. These freaky-looking fish have frills that fool other animals into thinking they are seaweed. They move slowly, sucking prey into their straw-like mouths.

PICK UP A PENGUIN

Look who's come for tea! A killer whale has dropped by for a feast—a tasty penguin snack! These mighty mammals can flip blocks of ice over, so penguins and seals are caught unawares and fall off!

Sargassum fish look just like seaweed. They lie in wait for crustaceans and small fish, although they have been known to eat fish as big as themselves!

Peculiar-looking cuttlefish can create flashes of color to dazzle their predators, or change color to blend in with their surroundings. If all that fails, these mollusks can disappear in a cloud of ink.

A saltwater crocodile can swim far out to sea. It grabs its prey with teeth that grow over 5 inches long, and holds it underwater until it drowns.

Shoals of mackerel fish dart, twist, and turn together in a group. Their scales reflect light so that confused predators can't pick out a victim among the swirling, twinkling bodies.

HIDE AND SEEK

Fighting friends

Boxer crabs are the ocean's tough guys with a secret weapon that keeps them safe from predators: poisonous boxing gloves! These smart crustaceans grab hold of sea anemones in their claws and wave them around threateningly. Sea anemones have nasty stings, so predators keep clear of their tentacles. The sea anemones benefit from this strange friendship, too—crabs are such messy eaters they can collect crumbs and other bits of debris that fall out of the crab's mouth!

HIDE

Razor sharp

Razorfish swim in groups, upside down, with their heads pointing toward the seafloor. They look more like plants than predators.

Killer whales have teeth that are up to 4 inches long.

HUNT

Killer whales are smart—they hunt in family groups and can talk to one another in high-pitched sounds.

TOXIC SHOCK

A single taste of vile venom could be enough to kill you. Venom is poison that many animals have inside their bodies. It's a handy weapon in the fight to stay alive, but only if potential predators know you're carrying it around.

That's why many venomous animals like to advertise their highly toxic state with strong signals. Bright and bold colors, patterns, and spines all tell predators to keep a safe distance. Some predators, however, use venom to kill their prey. They like to keep their weapon of fast destruction under wraps until the last moment…

DEADLY ANEMONE

Sea anemones are related to jellyfish and, like their swimming cousins, they have stinging tentacles that contain venom. The venom is mostly used to stun or kill prey, but these animals also sting in self-defence.

POISON EATERS

Smart **sea slugs**, called nudibranchs, get their venom from the food they eat. They munch on poisonous corals, sponges, and sea anemones, and keep the venom or stings for themselves. Sea slugs wear bright colors to advertise their toxic skin.

STONY GROUND

Watch where you put your foot if you paddle in the warm clear waters of Southeast Asia. **Stonefish** lurk, hidden from view, on the seabed. They have venomous spines on their dorsal fins and they are the world's deadliest venomous fish.

TOXINS

Toxins, like poisons or venoms, are harmful. Something that contains toxins is described as toxic.

VENOMOUS SNAKE

A **beaked sea snake** is twice as deadly as any land snakes and has enough venom to kill 50 people. These swimming slitherers live in shallow water and are camouflaged, so humans often disturb them by accident.

GROUP OF KILLERS

A **Portuguese man o' war** may look like just one animal, but actually it's a whole colony of tiny stinging creatures that hang beneath a gas-filled balloon.

ROAR!

Don't ever square up to a **lionfish**. These brave animals have been known to attack humans, although they usually hunt small fish at night. One smack with a venomous spine is enough to stun the prey, so the lionfish can devour it.

35

SMART MOVES

Seawater is 830 times denser than air, and that makes moving through it quite an achievement. It's an effort that's worth making, though, as swimmers can go to new ocean locations, in search of food and mates.

Swimmers need lots of energy to get anywhere, which is why lots of marine animals just hang about instead! Many sea creatures are able to float in the ocean, or move up and down by controlling the amount of gas in their body. Others just go with the flow, and allow the sea currents to carry them to new places.

Slow motion

Maned seahorses are named after their lion-like mane of spines, but these fish don't have the big cat's speed. Seahorses have so little muscle power that they can scarcely swim at all and have to wrap their tail around seaweed, to stop any small current from carrying them away.

BIG WORD ALERT

DENSITY
The way that particles are packed inside a substance is called its density, and it is similar to weight. Water is denser, and heavier, than air.

The world's largest movement of animals—a migration—happens twice a day, every day, in the oceans. Under the cover of darkness, billions and billions of plankton swim up to the Sunlight Zone to feast on the tiny plants that grow there. When the sun rises, they swim back down to the Twilight or Dark Zones, and hide from predators.

Hold on!
Every year, thousands of spiny lobsters grab hold of their friends in front to make one enormous line of marching crustaceans on the seabed. Each winter they migrate to deeper water—which is warmer and calmer than the shallow water near the shore at this time—to lay their eggs.

Fast forward

Sailfish can grow up to 11 feet long.

Sailfish are the fastest swimmers in the world.

They eat squid, octopus, and smaller fish such as sardines and anchovies.

They can reach speeds of 68 mph.

twist it!

WHAT A DRAG!

When an animal moves through water, the water particles push against it. This is called drag, and it slows movement right down.

Most sharks are slow swimmers, but the ferocious mako shark reaches top speeds of 55 mph.

Leatherback turtles are amazing long-distance swimmers. Using satellite-tracking systems, scientists discovered one turtle had swum 12,774 miles in a single migration!

Coconuts that fall into the sea can travel thousands of miles before coming to shore, where they might grow into new palm trees.

Deep sea lantern fish swim about a mile every night in a journey to the Sunlight Zone and back. That's like us running one-and-a-half marathons!

MOVE IT

SPEED LIMITS

Killer whale
34 mph

These enormous mammals can chase and kill animals even bigger than themselves.

California sea lion
25 mph

Fish swim fast, so sea lions need to be speedy to keep up with their lunch.

Gentoo penguins
23 mph

These birds almost fly underwater in short bursts when they are chasing their fishy prey.

MARINE MYSTERIES

Sailors, fishermen, swimmers, and explorers have all had good reason to fear the deep oceans. Far beneath the twinkling, rippling surface there could be all sorts of dangers, demons, or monsters lurking!

For thousands of years, people have reported spooky sounds, unexplained shipwrecks, and unrecognizable giant beasts at sea. Until recent times, it has been almost impossible to explore the underwater world, so people made up stories to explain any strange phenomena they encountered. There are usually good explanations for marine mysteries, but this huge habitat still holds many secrets.

MERMAIDS

The myth of mermaids has existed for thousands of years—even the great explorer Christopher Columbus believed he had seen several of them during his voyages. A mermaid is said to have the upper body of a woman, and the lower body of a fish. It's possible that this myth arose after people saw marine mammals, such as dugongs and manatees, from a distance.

Dr. J. Griffin pretended he got this small "mermaid" from Japanese fishermen when he brought it to New York in 1842. Crowds of curious visitors paid 25 cents each to see the marvel. Is it real or a fake?

UNSOLVED

INVESTIGATOR'S REPORT
Date: April 1918

Despite extensive searches, we are unable to find any sign of the USS *Cyclops*. This US Navy boat was lost at sea last month in a region known as the Bermuda Triangle, where other craft have mysteriously disappeared.

LOSSES: The whole crew (309 souls) is presumed lost at sea.

CAUSE: We are unable to establish cause of the disappearance of the ship. There is no wreckage and no distress signals were made.

CONCLUSION: The ship may have been bombed by wartime enemies, or sunk during a storm. However, there is no evidence to support either conclusion.

INVESTIGATOR'S REPORT
Date: January 1948

A Douglas DC-3 aircraft disappeared en route from Puerto Rico to Miami, passing through the Bermuda Triangle.

LOSSES: All 32 people on board are missing, presumed dead.

CAUSE: With no wreckage, and no survivors, it is impossible to say what caused the disappearance of the aircraft.

CONCLUSION: The pilot may not have received radio messages about a change in wind direction, causing him to get lost. Maybe he landed somewhere else safely? We will have to wait and see...

BIG WORD ALERT

CRYPTOZOOLOGIST
(say: krip-toe-zoo-olo-jist)
People who study stories of mysterious animals, such as Krakens (huge mythical sea monsters), and hope to find the truth behind the tales.

BLISTERING BARNACLES!

Something resembling a giant tentacled sea worm, more than 6 feet in length, alarmed locals when it washed ashore in Wales, UK, in 2009. Was it a mysterious marine monster that had been thrown up from the depths?

No, it actually turned out to be an unusually large colony of goose barnacles attached to an old ship's mast.

SOLVED

MYSTERY

SEA MONSTER

The following excerpt is taken from the diary of Jim Harris, a cabin boy on board HMS *Poseidon* in 1827. Does it prove the existence of sea monsters?

"Today we survived a most fearsome attack. The waves were billowing and the ship was pitching from side to side, when the Captain called all hands to deck. What a sight met our sorry eyes! A giant beast, the like of which I've never seen before, had grasped our vessel in its enormous tentacles, and threw us about like a leaf on a pond. We thought we were all done for. Suddenly, the heavens opened and a sheet of lightning ripped through the sky. The monster, which was most surely a kraken, took fright and fell beneath the waves. The Captain called us altogether for prayers of thanksgiving, but I'm too frightened to sleep tonight."

49

Ones to watch

Kraken (noun, mythological)
Said to be enormous sea monsters that resemble squid or octopuses and live in the seas near Norway and Iceland

Longman's beaked whale (noun)
Regarded as the world's most mysterious whale—until recently, no living ones had ever been seen, and scientists only knew they existed because two skulls had been found

bloop (noun)
Noise made by an unknown marine animal, first recorded underwater in 1997; no one has ever discovered what made them

globster (noun)
Dead body of an unidentified monster-like animal washed up on the shore; most globsters are big, jelly-like lumps and some are said to have shaggy hair

Red Devils (noun)
Once believed to be evil sea monsters by Mexican fishermen; have since been shown to be jumbo squid that dart through the water at lightning speed, and instantly change color from white to red when chased

DEEP-SEA EXPLORERS

THAT SINKING FEELING

For many explorers, the deep oceans present the world's last—and greatest—challenge. Every year, more people scale Mount Everest than climb into submarines to descend into the Abyss (see page 30).

Braving the depths is tough. Divers and explorers have to overcome a lack of oxygen, cold currents, and the weight of water bearing down on them.

Anyone wanting to go beyond a few hundred yards down needs to climb aboard an underwater vessel. It's a dangerous journey, but one that is rewarded by sights of incredible creatures. Are you ready to take the plunge?

In the 1940s, French diver Jacques Cousteau invented a way that divers could carry compressed air, in tanks on their backs. The system is known as SCUBA: Self-Contained Underwater Breathing Apparatus.

twist it!

DEEP THOUGHTS

Musician Katie Melua has played at nearly 1,000 feet below sea level with a band, on a platform oil rig in the North Sea.

The first diving suits were used in the 1830s. They were made of watertight rubber and canvas. Air was pumped from a boat above, through long tubes that were connected to the diver's metal helmet.

Robotic submersibles can explore the deep without putting any humans in danger. They are called Remotely Operated Vehicles, or ROVs for short.

The greatest undersea journey took place in 1960, when two explorers dived to 35,797 feet in a submersible called the *Trieste*. It took them about five hours to reach the bottom of the Mariana Trench in the Pacific Ocean.

The deepest any scuba diver has been able to go is 1,044 feet.

SUPERSUB!

Are you looking for an all-round vehicle with an extra thrill factor? Try the Dolphin and Seabreacher subs designed by Innespace of the USA. The fully enclosed vehicles can dive, jump, and roll, and travel up to 40 mph on the surface and 20 mph underwater.

40

People first began to explore the ocean depths just 200 years ago. They mostly went with shipwrecks, bad sunk in search of valuable cargo, such as gold, which

Diving can be a deadly pastime. If divers return to the surface too quickly, the change in water pressure can give them the bends, a potentially fatal condition.

Man's breath friend

Shadow is a scuba-diving dog that enjoys exploring underwater. He accompanies his owner, Dwane Folsom of the US, on scuba trips. Shadow wears his own special helmet and diving suit, and shares a breathing tube with Dwane.

Room with a view

If you're feeling rich and want to splash out on a hotel with a difference, check in at the Poseidon Underwater Hotel. Rooms will cost about $30,000 a week, but all guests get their own personal submarine to explore the underwater resort, plus a luxury room that sits 40 feet underwater, on the floor of a lagoon, with a view of the surrounding Fijian ocean life swimming by.

Ripley's Believe It or Not!®

UP ANCHOR!

Traveling across oceans sometimes requires great courage to combat the combined forces of wind, waves, currents, and the planet's fiercest weather.

Long ago, mariners sailed or rowed across the oceans in search of new lands and opportunities. They found their way by following the stars, but many of them lost their lives in storms and shipwrecks. Most modern journeys make use of the latest technology, including boats that are equipped with communication and satellite navigation systems. Some ocean journeys are even made in the lap of luxury, such as on the *Oasis of the Seas*!

The ship is 1,187 feet long and 208 feet wide.

FUN FEATURES

- Water and light show with 65-feet high fountains
- A zipwire stretched between nine decks
- An ice rink
- Diving platforms and a trapeze
- Carousels and funfair activities

It has 2,706 guest rooms, 16 decks, 24 elevators, and nearly 2,000 balconies.

SEA MONSTER

The world's largest passenger ship has been described as a holiday village in the ocean—but with 8,000 people on board it's more like a town! The *Oasis of the Seas* is so big it even has room for tropical gardens with 56 growing trees, a science lab, and basketball courts.

AQUALANDS

CENTRAL PARK

ROYAL PROMENADE

Guests on the *Oasis* enjoy the chilling effects of 110,231 pounds of ice cubes every day.

CAROUSEL

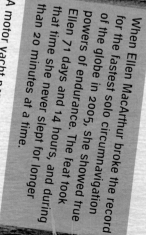

BIG
WORD ALERT

CIRCUMNAVIGATION
A circumnavigation is a journey all the way around something. It usually refers to a sea voyage all the way around the world.

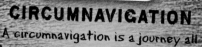
twist it!

A motor yacht named *Dubai* was built for one of the world's richest men. It is so large there's room for a helicopter pad, cinema, gym, and squash court. It even has its own submarine!

When Ellen MacArthur broke the record for the fastest solo circumnavigation of the globe in 2005, she showed true powers of endurance. The feat took Ellen 71 days and 14 hours, and during that time she never slept for longer than 20 minutes at a time.

SEAFARERS
The first people to row across the Atlantic Ocean were George Harbo and Frank Samuelson of Norway. It took them nearly two months to row 3,270 miles in 1896.

TREASURE TROVE

The oceans and seas cover most of the Earth's surface. They are home to billions of living things, and contribute to the planet's health in many different ways. People have been relying on the oceans' rich produce for thousands of years.

Oceans provide food for billions of people around the world, as well as jobs for the people who catch fish. Long ago, people fished for just the food they needed, but now too many fish are being taken from the sea. Too little is being done to protect marine habitats, and too much garbage is being thrown into the oceans. There is some good news though, people all over the world are working hard to save our seas and create special places where ocean wildlife is safe.

SEAFOOD SHORTAGE

Tuna is one of the world's favorite fish to eat. In recent years, 95 percent of all bluefin tuna have been removed from the sea, and they could disappear completely soon.

Nearly half of all known types of animals and plants live in oceans.

FOOD FOR THOUGHT

The Inuit people of the Arctic enjoy a type of walrus meat called *igunaaq*. It is stored under a pile of stones and, over the course of one year, it freezes and thaws so many times it becomes a rotting, stinking mass. Yum!

Most countries of the world have agreed not to hunt whales for meat any more, but seven species of great whales are still in danger of dying out forever.

Ermis and Androniki Nicholas love fish and chips so much they travel 60 miles every day to the coast for a fish lunch; and they have been making this trip for ten years!

A high-energy drink on sale in Japan is made from... eels! It's yellow, fizzy, and still has the fish heads and bones in it.

twist it!

Pretty wasteful

Pieces of coral, seashells, and sea creatures are used to make souvenirs and sold to tourists all over the world. Pearls and sponges are also harvested from the sea. Many animals are killed and their habitats destroyed for this trade.

ANTARCTIC ANTIFREEZE

Fish that live in the icy Antarctic are able to survive thanks to special antifreeze chemicals in their bodies. They work by locking up ice crystals, to stop them from spreading. Scientists hope to copy the chemicals and make antifreeze paint for aircraft wings.

Doctors are using zebrafish and horseshoe crabs in an attempt to discover new medicines and repair damaged human hearts.

Some wind farms are located offshore so they can get maximum benefit from the strong gales that blow over the surface of the oceans.

JELLYFISH NOODLES

Scientists believe that the best way to make sure we don't use up all of the fish in the sea for food is to create marine reserves—areas in the oceans where no one is allowed to fish. Then, the endangered fish would be able to breed in these areas and increase their numbers once more. If we don't do this, some people believe that the only creatures left in the sea in large numbers for us to eat will be jellyfish! Jellyfish noodles, anyone?

RICH RESOURCES

The world's oceans provide a great deal of the energy we use in our everyday lives. Offshore platforms extract oil and natural gas from beneath the seabed, but one day these fuels, which are used to make power, will run out. New technology can harness the power of the wind and the waves to make electricity. These wind and wave farms provide a renewable, or never-ending, source of power that could give the world some of its energy in the future. Phew!

45

INDEX

ACKNOWLEDGMENTS

COVER David Fleetham/Taxi/Getty Images, (b/r) Greenpeace/Rex Features

2 (t) © nata_rass – Fotolia.com, (b) © javarman – Fotolia.com; **3** (t) Jim Morgan jmorgan8@cfl.rr.com, (r) Robert Innes; **4** (c) David Fleetham/Taxi/Getty Images; **4–5** (b) © aleksander1 – Fotolia.com; **6** (t, t/r) © Stephen Rees – iStock.com; **6–7** © Ramon Purcell – iStock.com; **7** (t/r) NASA/GSFC, MODIS Rapid Response; **8** (t/l, t/c, t/r) NASA/GSFC, MODIS Rapid Response; **8–9** Igor Liberti www.apnea.ch; **9** (t/r, b/r, b) U.S. Navy Photo; **10** (l) © Paul Allen – Fotolia.com, (b/c) Suzi Eszterhas/Minden Pictures/FLPA, (b/cl) Matthias Breiter/Minden Pictures/FLPA, (b/cr) © Lynn M. Stone, (b/l) © Oceans Image/Photoshot, (c/l) © NHPA/Photoshot; **11** (b/r, t/r) © NHPA/Photoshot (sp) © Alberto Pomares – iStock.com; **12–13** (c) Constantinos Petrinos/Nature Picture Library/Rex Features; **13** (t/r) Jeff Rotman/Naturepl.com, (c/r) Jim Morgan jmorgan8@cfl.rr.com, (b/r) David Fleetham/Bluegreenpictures.com; **14** (c) © Oceans Image/Photoshot, (b/l) © Monty Chandler – Fotolia.com; **14–15** (dp) © John Anderson – iStock.com, (b) David Espin – Fotolia.com; **15** (t/r) © Piero Malaer – iStock.com, (c/r) © Richard Carey – Fotolia.com, (b/r) Barcroft Media via Getty Images; **16–17** (dp) Jim Edds/Science Photo Library; **17** (c) Marlin.ac.uk/stevetrewhella@hotmail.com, (c/r) © David Fleetham/Bluegreenpictures.com, (b/r) © a_elmo – Fotolia.com, (b) © Mark Carwadine/naturepl.com; **18** (t/l) © pipehorse – Fotolia.com, (t/c) Georgette Douwma/Science Photo Library, (t/r) © Richard Carey – Fotolia.com; **18–19** Doug Perrine/Bluegreenpictures.com; **19** (t/l) © Richard Carey – Fotolia.com, (t/c) © nata_rass – Fotolia.com, (t/r) Birgit Koch/Imagebroker/FLPA, (c) P. Bush/Barcroft Media Ltd (b/r) Tommy Schultz – Fotolia.com; **20** (b/l) ImageBroker/Imagebroker/FLPA; **20–21** Gary Meszaros/Science Photo Library; **21** (t/r) © Oceans Image/Photoshot, (c) Michael Nolan/Splashdowndirect/Rex Features, (b/r) Greenpeace/Rex Features; **22** © Reinhard Dirscherl/FLPA; **23** (c) Brandon Cole/Bluegreenimages.com, (b/l) D.J. Struntz/Barcroft Media Ltd; **24** (t/r) International Antartic Centre, (t/c) California Academy of Sciences, (b/l) © javarman – Fotolia.com, (b/c) © Sergey Korotkov – iStock.com, (b/r) © Eric Isselée – Fotolia.com; **25** (c) Andy Rouse/Rex Features, (r) Ingo Arndt/Minden Pictures/FLPA, (b/l) iStock.com, (b/c) © Paul Tessier – iStock.com, (b/r) © Iain Sarjeant – iStock.com; **26** (t, b/l) © NHPA/Photoshot; **27** (t) Barry Bland/Barcroft Media Ltd, (b/r) © Nancy Nehring – iStock.com; **28** (t/r) Dreamstime.com, (c) © idy – Fotolia.com, (b/l) Quirky China/Rex Features; **28–29** (dp) © Ferran Traite Soler – iStock.com; **29** (t) © Alan James/Naturepl.com, (c) © Francesca Rizzo – iStock.com, (b) David Fleetham/Bluegreenpictures.com; **30** (b/l, b/r) David Shale/Bluegreenpictures.com; **30–31** (t) © Frans Lanting/Corbis, (c) © NHPA/Photoshot; **31** (b/r) David Shale/Bluegreenpictures.com; **32** (t) © Oceans-Image/Photoshot, (l) © Scott McCabe – iStock.com, (c/l) © Florian Graner/Naturepl.com; **32–33** (b) Norbert Wu/Minden Pictures/FLPA; **33** (t/r) David B Fleetham/PhotoLibrary, (c) © Markus Koller – Fotolia.com; **34** (t) © Kerry Werry – iStock.com, (b/l) © Achim Prill – iStock.com, (b/r) © John Anderson – iStock.com; **34–35** (dp) pablo del rio sotelo – iStock.com; **35** (t, c/r) © NHPA/Photoshot, (b) © Jacob Wackerhausen – iStock.com; **36** (t) © NHPA/Photoshot, (b) © Doug Perrine/naturepl.com; **37** (t) © Doug Perrine/Bluegreenpictures.com, (b/r) © aleksander1 – Fotolia.com; **38** (b) Rex Features (r) United States Naval History and Heritage Command photograph; **38–39** (dp) © Kevin Russ – iStock.com; **39** (t/l) iStock.com, (t/r) Professor Paul Brain/Wenn.com, (c) Time & Life Pictures/Getty Images, (b) © Stefanie Leuker – Fotolia.com; **40** (t) Robert Innes; **40–41** (c) © Robert Nu/FLPA; **41** (t/r, c/r) Rex Features, (b) Palm Beach Post/Rex Features; **42–43** KPA/Zuma/Rex Features; **44** Wild Wonders of Europe/Zankl/Bluegreenpictures.com; **45** (t) Norbert Wu/Minden Pictures/FLPA, (t/r) © Sean Gladwell – Fotolia.com, (b) Photolibrary.com/photofactory, (b/r) © Francesca Rizzo – iStock.com, (r) Woodfall Wild Images/Photoshot

Key: t = top, b = bottom, c = center, l = left, r = right, sp = single page, dp = double page, bgd = background
All other photos are from Ripley Entertainment Inc. All artwork by Rocket Design (East Anglia) Ltd.

Every attempt has been made to acknowledge correctly and contact copyright holders and we apologize in advance for any unintentional errors or omissions, which will be corrected in future editions.

TWISTS